LIVING on
PURPOSE
JOURNEY TO DISCOVERING WHY

DR. MARY E. ADAMS

LIVING on PURPOSE
JOURNEY TO DISCOVERING WHY

XULON PRESS

Xulon Press
2301 Lucien Way #415
Maitland, FL 32751
407.339.4217
www.xulonpress.com

Unless otherwise indicated, Scripture quotations taken from Scripture quotations taken from the Holy Bible, New International Version (NIV). Copyright © 1973, 1978, 1984, 2011 by Biblica, Inc.™. Used by permission. All rights reserved.

Scripture quotations taken from the New King James Version (NKJV). Copyright © 1982 by Thomas Nelson, Inc. Used by permission. All rights reserved.

Scripture quotations taken from The Message (MSG). Copyright © 1993, 1994, 1995, 1996, 2000, 2001, 2002. Used by permission of NavPress Publishing Group. Used by permission. All rights reserved.

Printed in the United States of America.

ISBN-13: 978-1-54565-219-0

Dedication

In memory of parents, Thomas and Edna McLaurin, who instilled many valuable lessons that are continuously impacting my life.

Contents

Acknowledgements

How do I say thanks to God for the many lessons learned along the journey? All glory and honor to Him for amazing love, faithfulness and compassion in every season of life.

To family, both natural and spiritual, ministry team, friends, colleagues, those who have given support in prayer and given words of encouragement, thank you very much. A very special thanks to my husband, Rob who for nearly 50 years, has always been a great cheerleader and supporter of all personal and ministry endeavors.

Then He said to His disciples, "The harvest truly is plentiful, but the laborers are few. Therefore, pray the Lord of the harvest to send out laborers into His harvest."

(Matthew 9:37-38)

But the hour is coming, and now is, when the true worshipers will worship the Father in spirit and truth; for the Father is seeking such to worship Him. God is Spirit, and those who worship Him must worship in spirit and truth.

(John 4:23-24)

Introduction

For many years, the search for life's purpose and why I was born involved a great deal of time, energy and resources. There are certainly motives behind everything that is done; therefore, discovering the reason for being here is critical for learning how to live on purpose. The endeavor to become a diligent seeker of life's meaning helped to navigate the journey during many seasons of trials, uncertainties and to identify my unique purpose. The preparation process, however, took a very long time but at the end of the day, benefits received paled in comparison to the seasons of struggle. Learning to live on purpose and knowing why can be helpful for becoming secure in your identity. The confidence in knowing that you are approved by God and not people brings great joy and peace. Everyone has a story to tell, but each story is distinct because no one else has had the same challenges or struggles in the same way. There are elements in each story that definitively identify passion and purpose, making one not better than anyone else, but different.

Although each individual's life is unique, they grow and develop through the same basic sequence. The course of one's life involves a complex process in which there are qualitatively different phases or seasons. Change occurs in every season that requires transitional shifting from one to another. Success is no accident. It is difficult work that demands perseverance, learning, studying, sacrifice and most importantly, love of what you are doing. Expectation is the breeding ground of great achievements; therefore, you will get whatever is prepared for and expected.

Beginning this book project, which evolved from lunchtime conversations with dear friends, is proving to be very exciting. It is a great honor to share a great friendship with some phenomenal ladies who are encouraging and motivating. So, at their suggestion, I was requested to write a spiritual perspective concerning living on purpose and the discovery process of personal belief system. Although a published author of several books, working on this project is very stimulating as I reflect upon experiences of publishing the first book many years ago.

Please understand that any achievements, accolades and successes gained throughout life's journey were not because of being certain of purpose or why I was here. For the most part, just happened to be in the right place, at the right time, with the right people. As many lessons were learned during some heartbreaking or challenging situations, a decision was made, very early in life, to seek God's help and guidance. Consequently, it's been an exhilarating ride of a lifetime. Herein are some details about the quest to discover life's purpose and why I am serving in the kingdom, for such a time as this. Hopefully, you will find this reading to be helpful, encouraging and inspirational on your quest to live on purpose.

Chapter I

Pursuing Purpose

No one has all the answers concerning how to successfully achieve desired goals; nonetheless, after several decades of learning life's lessons, here are some questions to be answered that can help you along your journey:

- What's my current situation?
- Who am I?
- Where do I want to go?
- Am I willing to risk change to become better?
- Will I commit to begin where I am?

Everyone has a story to tell, but each story is distinct because no one else has had the same challenges or struggles in the same way. There are elements in each story that definitively identify passion and purpose, making one not better than anyone else, but different. Although each individual's life is unique, everyone goes through the same basic sequence. The course of one's life involves a complex process in which there are qualitatively different phases or seasons. Change occurs in every season that requires transitional shifting from one to another.

During times of confronting some heart wrenching situations, I began the quest to discover life's purpose. These were times of confusion, anxiousness, discouragement with so many questions about divine purpose. Having a consistent prayer life was essential for helping to navigate through many stormy and difficult seasons. Throughout seasons of enduring under tremendous pressure, I am continuously learning to trust and stand firmly on God's promises. It is often said: into each life, some rain must fall; however, depending upon one's unique life's purpose, a little rain can turn into raging floods, along with some dark and catastrophic circumstances.

In 2001, after dealing with a myriad of struggles, journaling became the vehicle used for writing about personal life's experiences. Based upon the premise that others could benefit from these experiences, decided to share in the book project <u>Beneath the Surface</u>, an auto-biographical account of these struggles. Some details are provided about how prayer, believing and trusting God provided strength and directions during various traumatic seasons. At that time, however, didn't consider myself an author; but rather just wanted to share the reason for being passionate about pursuing a personal relationship with Christ.

Insecurities experienced during challenging times help to define who you really are at the core and discovering your why. You are challenged, for the most part, in chaos and not in comfort. From this perspective, you can learn over time, that surviving through several challenging situations are helpful for discovering life's purpose. In overcoming stormy seasons, you are given an opportunity to cooperate with God as you learn to live on purpose.

Now God has us where he wants us, with all the time in this world and the next to shower grace and kindness upon us in Christ Jesus. Saving is all his idea, and all his work. All we do is trust him enough to let him do it. It's God's gift from start to finish! We don't play the major role. If we did, we'd probably go around bragging that we'd done the whole thing! No, we neither make nor save ourselves. God does both the making and saving. He creates each of us by Christ Jesus to join him in the work he does, the good work he has gotten ready for us to do, work we had better be doing. (Ephesians 2:7-10)

It is not wise to take for granted whenever there is a successful outcome in a particular season because things can change on a dime. Unexpected turbulence for example: death of a loved one, sickness, natural disaster, relationship or financial crisis, etc., can make the journey discouraging, disappointing, bumpy, uncertain and unpleasant. As a result, it is critical for survival to fasten your seat belt, stay focused, praying always, stand your ground confidently in faith and ride out uncomfortable times.

He who believes in Me as the scriptures have said, out of him shall flow rivers of living waters (John 7:38). Everything lives wherever the river flows (Ezekiel 47:9).

No matter how dead or dry a situation may become, you can speak life and begin again. Regardless of the difficulties of past experiences, it's not over until God says it's over. Evaluate what you have left and keep moving forward in pursuit of your destiny. If you are developing an intimate relationship with God, just know that He's more than enough to provide grace in abundance, as trials grow greater. Seek Him for strategies to strengthen whatever remains so that you can continue moving forward in victory. Over time, amid many situations, faith level increases, to the extent, your divine purpose as a change agent is clarified.

Don't let current situations or circumstances dampen your pursuit for fulfilling life's purpose. Against the backdrop of so much turmoil, confusion, darkness all around, God still reigns and speaks peace to the faithful. In other words, don't be anxious about uncomfortable situations, trust God and leave the outcome to Him.

God is the answer to the problems of the world; therefore, be still and know that He is God (Psalm 46:10). Rest and wait patiently for Him (Psalm 37:7). He is the light of the world, in Him, there is kindness and no darkness. You were called, chosen to share in His eternal glory by means of Christ Jesus and to produce good fruit in your spheres of influence (John 15:16).

So, after you have suffered a little while, He will restore, support, strengthen and place you on a firm foundation. All power to Him forever!

(1 Peter 5:10-11).

And I am certain that God, who began the good work within you, will continue his work until it is finally finished on the day when Christ Jesus returns. (Philippians 1:6)

After spending years in search of God's purpose, lessons learned prompted teaching, mentoring and writing to encourage others, especially ministry leaders, who are also pursuing their divine purpose. Having something to believe in-and discovering 'Why' became instrumental for teaching, preaching and writing to share information that was garnered throughout many years of experience. Everyone has a purpose for being here; however, the journey of discovery is a very long and arduous process.

For I know the plans I have for you, says the Lord. "They are plans for good and not for disaster, to give you a future and a hope." (Jeremiah 29:11)

Chapter II

Identifying Purpose

The Spirit of the Sovereign Lord is upon me, for the Lord has anointed me to bring good news to the poor. He has sent me to comfort the brokenhearted and to proclaim that captives will be released and prisoners will be freed. He has sent me to tell those who mourn that the time of the Lord's favor has come, and with it, the day of God's anger against their enemies. To all who mourn in Israel, he will give a crown of beauty for ashes, a joyous blessing instead of mourning, festive praise instead of despair. In their righteousness, they will be like great oaks that the Lord has planted for his own glory. (Isaiah 61:1-3)

Ministry Focus Points:

Love God-Love People (John 3:16).

Go into all the world, preach the gospel, make disciples of others being assured that God is with you until the end of the age (Matthew 28:19-20).

1. Help others to know that the power of God saves, heals, delivers and sets free.
2. Identify internal issues to be addressed: rebellion, disobedience, envy, strife, oppression, shame, pride, laziness, greed, selfishness, insecurities, depression, etc.
3. Appropriate Response: Repent, surrender wholeheartedly, submit to instructions given during training and developmental process.

In the quest to discover your 'WHY' for identifying purpose, the growth and developmental process can be very challenging. At the end of the day, however, you finally learn to embrace seasonal challenges and how to manage changes effectively. Whenever expectations inevitably collide with disappointment, lessons learned are helpful for navigating through uncharted waters.

Life is a journey, not a destination in which there's an opportunity, on many occasions, to discover why you were born. The journey, more often than not, may seem to be a simple endeavor, however, discovering your unique purpose can be an arduous process. Nonetheless, from a spiritual perspective, this feat can be successfully accomplished by utilizing certain foundational biblical principles. As long as the earth remains, seed-time-harvest-day-night and seasons will not cease (Genesis 8:22). Along the way, you learn that there are very few absolutes, such as: the law of gravity, aerodynamics and law of reciprocity. In other words, what goes up must come down and you reap whatever is sown.

According to the Divine plan, you did not show up on the earth by accident, even-though circumstances surrounding your birth may have been very unpleasant or undesirable. In order to live on purpose, it is vital to have something you can believe in that is motivating, inspiring and enjoyable. Every life has a unique purpose; therefore, you have a story that no one else can tell. It is clearly stated in the word of God, that you were placed on earth to fulfill a specific purpose (Jeremiah 29:11; Psalm 139:13-16; Ephesians 2:10). Identifying purpose is essential for learning to live on purpose so that you can enjoy life and see beauty in every season.

Chapter III

Turning Points

O n life's journey, there are many turning points, a time when decisive changes are made. In these times of unrest, violence, social/moral decline and disasters of epic proportions, it appears, in some people's opinion, that the church is proving to be ineffective. It seems in many ways, that love and compassion for others are growing cold. The harvest is great but the laborers are few (Matthew 9:35-38).

In these times, there is an urgent need to pray for revival, renewal, refreshing, igniting the fire of passion, fan the flame, awaken gifts and return to your first love (2 Timothy 1:5-7; Revelation 2:2-5). Turning points provide an opportunity to rise up, move forward and earnestly contend for the faith entrusted to the Lord's church. You are called and chosen to spread the good news of salvation, for such a time as this.

Jesus stated, "Why are you so polite with Me, always saying 'Yes, sir,' and 'That's right, sir,' but never doing a thing I tell you? These words I speak to you are not mere additions to your life, homeowner improvements to your standard of living. They are foundation words, words to build a life on. If you work the words into your life, you are like a smart carpenter who dug deep and laid the foundation of his house on bedrock. When the river burst its banks and crashed against the house, nothing could shake it; it was built to last. But if you just use My words in Bible studies and don't work them into your life, you are like a dumb carpenter who built a house but skipped the foundation. When the swollen river came crashing in, it collapsed like a house of cards. It was a total loss. (Luke 6:46-49)

You can recognize a turning point whenever there's an inner knowing that everything prayed for, sown into and waited patiently for is about to come to pass. God Himself had decided long ago, at what point a change needed to take place in your life. Turning points are often preceded by times of intense prayer, meditation and consecration; wherein, an increase of power and authority are provided for a specific assignment.

During seasons of preparation and consecration, at times you may experience feelings of shame, disappointment and humiliation; however, at the same time God releases an inner knowing that victory is near! With all this in mind, it is important to recognize that the new place you are being ushered into calls for drawing a line in the sand. This is essential for discerning who and what God authorizes at this particular time and season.

You cannot allow distractions of any kind or negativity distance you from your unique divine assignment. Stay focused, focused, focused! Opportunities will come and go quickly; therefore, timing is everything! Being at the right place, at the right time, with the right people are essential. The promises God made to you do not have an expiration date or become null and void! They only have conditions, such as: diligently seek the kingdom and its righteousness-stop waiting for someone else to prophesy and give an interpretation of the conditions that are necessary for the promises of God to be fulfilled in your life.

It's imperative to get rid of an impatient mindset and remain faithful while you are waiting for God, but at the same time, embrace changes that are being made. When God commands movement, there is no time for negotiation, interpretation or outside revelation. Just move whenever He says move and stay in step! Going ahead of God is dangerous and lagging behind because of fear is not advised.

God is releasing a spirit of urgency over His people to align their lives with His purposes and plans. This is a time of reversal and recovery in that God is about to grant access to people, places and things that until now, have not been accessible. Make sure to have on turning point garments and be ready to impact the kingdom of God with necessary changes, for such a time as this!

Jesus' earthly ministry began a revolution of love and compassion that continues to significantly impact every generation. Through the power of the Holy Spirit, He demonstrates unconditional love, healing and deliverance to those who are sick, broken, marginalized or oppressed by the devil. The gospel of love and reconciliation have continued to be taught by faithful believers over time, despite seasons of martyrdom and severe persecution in every generation. You can believe that things are turning around in your favor, in due time and season! As a carrier of good news, you can shout it out from the rooftops that the love of God is amazing, His mercy is everlasting.

Don't panic in the face of tests, trials; stand firm on God's word, being confident that everything needed is already provided. Whenever you call on the name of the Lord, He will answer prayer and guide you on the journey from promises revealed to promises fulfilled. Seasons of change involve a transitional process, from narrow or tight places, to a larger place of blessing.

There are times/seasons of bearing under intense pain/pressure, being stretched, tested and challenged on every hand; however, at the end of the day, you are empowered and refreshed by the Holy Spirit to move forward into a brand- new beginning.

Weeping endures in the night season but joy comes at the breaking of a new day! There is always encouragement, direction and hope for a bright future in the word of God.

Enlarge the place of your tent, stretch your tent curtains wide, do not hold back; lengthen your cords, strengthen your stakes. For you will spread out to the right and to the left; your descendants will dispossess nations and settle in their desolate cities. (Isaiah 54:2-3)

Life lessons: Desired goals attained in life, are preceded by long periods of intense preparation, persistence and perseverance, just as in the birthing process. In this process there are periods of pain, pushing, pressure, moaning and travail. The pressing place is a time of being alone. Although others may be present during the labor and delivery process, they cannot feel what you feel.

Here's another example of an intense preparation process: A goal of being prepared to perform with a symphony orchestra requires years of specialized training, discipline, dedication, determination, opportunities and connections.

Nuggets on Turning Points:

- **New levels of refreshing and revelation are released**
- **Current vision is adjusted, secured, established for greater impact**
- **Fleshly props are removed by fresh wind blowing**
- **Mantle of restoration is placed to aid in healing process of past experiences**
- **You are given a new identity with confidence and courage**

- Fresh strategies are revealed with vision of possessing greater territory
- You are provided with strength to outlast/overthrow enemies

Miracles begin to happen whenever you choose to embrace changes resulting from critical events and surrender wholeheartedly to God's will. Structure and order are necessary for progressing into another dimension that's not driven by emotional needs. You can choose to renovate and stay committed to a prayer life in order to deal with additional stressors. Faith is a commitment to believe and trust God in every situation or circumstance. Although a promised move of God is preceded by times of great opposition, however, life's contradictions are the criteria for greatness. In other words, it is a conflict between realities in your life and where you desire to be.

Signs of God's presence amid difficult situations demonstrate that you are victorious, despite weakness. His grace is sufficient in all seasons.

During seasons of fighting for the faith, being discouraged and feeling like quitting, very often are indicators that breakthrough is imminent. Many challenges are all around, yet God is working within faithful and available servants who choose to rise to the occasion. As you embrace changes occurring at a turning point, from lessons learned, a significant impact can be made within areas of influence that will affect succeeding generations.

In a comfort and convenience minded environment, no one wants to hear that it is necessary to endure difficult times as a precursor to achieving a successful outcome in life. Those who have availed themselves to following a righteous path will suffer persecution (Acts 14:22). However, the place of suffering at the merciful hands of adverse situations, become the crucible for revealing a Christ centered life.

Along the way, there are so many nuggets you can chew on to help keep you focused such as:

- **Power of Choice**
- **Confidence-Courage-Capable-Change Manager**
- **Committed to Prayer-Worship-Study**

In difficult times, resolve to adjust to blowing of fresh winds, recognizing that change can either crush or propel you forward. Pain, uncomfortable and tight places become the wind that fuel destiny in an extraordinary way. From life's experiences you can find your unique voice and share hope/encouragement with others who are struggling in similar situations. There is always a need for God's available army to continue building up the kingdom; therefore, it is a privilege and honor to hear and obey His voice.

Then He said to me, "Prophesy to these bones, and say to them, 'Dry bones, hear the word of the Lord!' This is what the Sovereign Lord says to these bones: "I will make breath enter you, and you will come to life." (Ezekiel 37:4-5)

Kingdom Principles:

- **Seed-Time-Harvest**
- **Team Approach**
- **Build on solid foundation**
- **Diligently seek the Lord**
- **God uses broken, empty vessels**
- **Surrender wholeheartedly**
- **Launch out deeper in faith**
- **Choose the right response**

- Learn the integrity of what God has placed in you
- Great oppositions showcase the power and glory of God

Many adverse situations are all around, yet God is working within faithful, willing and obedient servants. They are being led by the Holy Spirit to rise to the occasion and move forward out of comfort zones into an uncharted territory! Now is the time and season to call on God wholeheartedly, asking for mercy. Expect unexpected things to happen because opposition helps you learn the integrity of what God has placed within. Sometimes enemies sow tares among good seed, however, choose to draw closer and accept divine destiny (Matthew 13:25; 1 Peter 4:12, 5:10).

There is healing, freedom and deliverance in the presence of the Lord; therefore, you can cross over all hindrances or obstacles into greater dimensions. Amid life's turning point, everything changes and shifts, repositioning you to a new place.

Chapter IV

Available for Service

I n writing this chapter, I am reflecting upon a specific time when wholehearted surrender to the Lord occurred, as a result, the decision was made to become available and obedient to His will. Although this was not a one-time event, very important lessons were learned concerning the high cost of making yourself available for kingdom service. At this particular time, some very difficult and challenging circumstances had left me feeling overwhelmed, to the extent, my soul cried out to God for help and deliverance. Needless to say, the amazing love of God reached the hurt, pain and grief lodged deep beneath the surface and lifted me out of despair. He gave me overflowing joy and peace that words cannot explain; therefore, all that I am and ever hope to be is for His glory.

Maybe you can relate to having similar experiences. It's a time when adverse situations make you sick and tired of being sick and tired of going around in circles, looking for love and acceptance.

God is faithful to heal, save and deliver the soul that cries out to Him for help; He revives, restores and refreshes over and over again. The book of Psalms speaks volumes concerning God's response to the cries of a soul in distress (Psalm 3:4, 18:6, 34:4, 118:5, 120:1). As you continue being available for kingdom service, God is faithful to help you navigate through multiple challenges along the way.

So do not fear, for I am with you; do not be dismayed, for I am your God. I will strengthen you and help you; I will uphold you with my righteous right hand. (Isaiah 41:10)

Have I not commanded you? Be strong and courageous. Do not be terrified; do not be discouraged, for the Lord, your God will be with you wherever you go. (Joshua 1:9)

Know that the Lord is strong and mighty to rescue His people from dangerous situations; He is well able to do above and beyond what you ask or think according to the power working at your core (Ephesians 3:20). In order to stay on the right track, it is very important to maintain fresh perspectives; in other words, pay attention to what you see and hear. Don't ever forget past victories of how the Lord delivered you from the power of darkness. Be assured, fully convinced and persuaded that He is able to keep everything together and bring you into fulfillment of His purpose. If you are willing and obedient, you will be prosperous and successful.

You are called and chosen to be fruitful; therefore, it's necessary to be available to endure the painful process of growth and development. Remember God created you for purpose and ensures the completion of the good work He began.

You did not choose Me, but I chose you and appointed you that you should go and bear fruit, and that your fruit should remain, that whatever you ask the Father in My name He may give you. These things I command you, that you love one another. (John 15:16-17)

Here are some points to consider if you are available for kingdom service:

1. Surrender wholeheartedly to obeying God's purpose for your life.

2. Be strong and courageous; do not be afraid; trust, obey and meditate on His word.

3. Be confident and assured of success and prosperity, knowing that God has called, chosen and anointed you for a specific assignment.

4. He will never leave or forsake you; He is with you to bring success in every endeavor along the journey.

5. Prepare for crossing over into a new territory; be sensitive to God's timing and season.

6. Follow directions of designated leader.

When all you have is God, He is all you need and more than enough. He is able to do far above imagination or thoughts. His love is limitless, has no boundaries, goes beyond religiosity, legalism, societal/cultural norms and all types of systems to bring healing and deliverance to those who are sick or oppressed (Acts 10:38). His Love exists throughout time and eternity; He is faithful and in Him, there is no variableness or darkness (John 3:16; 1John 3:16; 1John 4:10).

Love is as love does, is not pity but shows compassion for those who are bruised, broken or sick. There is a difference between pity and compassion. Those who have experienced pain and suffering can appreciate other's suffering and show compassion or empathy. Disciples of Christ are obedient followers of His example to exhibit love and compassion toward others.

As the image of Christ is developed, there is less room to showcase yourself. He is not impressed with performance- based religion, but is interested in you cultivating a personal relationship with Him. Being available to complete assignments exceptionally well meets His approval (Matthew 25:23; Luke 16:10).

It is so very important to be aware of generational curses and its effect on your present realities. Your perception of ancestral traumas within a cultural environment gets passed down to children through their bloodline. The way you think about past traumas can be formative, therefore it can significantly impact behavior.

By faith, you can be confident and fully persuaded of being more than a conqueror through Christ because there is nothing that can separate you from His love. Know that the Lord is strong and mighty to rescue you and your children from generational curses or any dangerous situations. At the end of the day, it is better to trust and obey God in everything. Resolve to do things His way knowing that the end justifies the means; therefore, you can expect a mighty move of God in the right season. Are you available to spread the good news that Jesus saves, heals, delivers and set free?

How beautiful on the mountains are the feet of those who bring good news, who proclaim peace, who bring good tidings, who proclaim salvation, who say to Zion, "Your God reigns!" (Isaiah 52:7)

Chapter V

Choices

To a certain degree, each person is shaped by cultural norms and values within the environment in which they are born. For many, this is a good thing; however, as a child I didn't like the circumstances that surrounded being born into a poverty-stricken community. The family environment consisted of nine siblings, along with some cousins who were all struggling together in the same house to survive on limited resources. As a result, the endeavor to overcome this situation was very challenging on several fronts. Of course, didn't realize at the time that amid some chaotic times, these events were instrumental in the preparation process for fulfilling my specific purpose in destiny.

The ending of a thing is better than its beginning; therefore, the end justifies the means. Every challenge, seasonal difficulty, continuously proves that God reigns in the midst of it all. Trusting in His faithfulness and love encourages and restores the soul. I realize that divine assistance, during life's challenging experiences, served as a tool for discovering life's purpose.

As a catalyst of change, it is essential to experience change firsthand by working on your own flaws. You can't change the past but from lessons learned, it's your choice to have an exceptional, productive and enjoyable life. Change is inevitable but growth is optional-it's your choice. Every day, you can choose to be better or bitter, thankful or ungrateful and see the beauty in every season. No matter the difficulty of situations, you can choose to say: Yes; It is well; not my will Lord but Yours be done.

I'm not saying that I have this all together, that I have it made. But I am well on my way, reaching out for Christ, who has so wondrously reached out for me. Friends, don't get me wrong: By no means do I count myself an expert in all of this, but I've got my eye on the goal, where God is beckoning us onward—to Jesus. I'm off and running, and I'm not turning back. So let's keep focused on that goal, those of us who want everything God has for us. If any of you have something else in mind, something less than total commitment, God will clear your blurred vision—you'll see it yet! Now that we're on the right track, let's stay on it. Stick with me, friends. Keep track of those you see running this same course, headed for this same goal. There are many out there taking other paths, choosing other goals, and trying to get you to go along with them. I've warned you of them many times; sadly, I'm having to do it again. All they want is easy street. They hate Christ's Cross. But easy street is a dead-end street. Those who live there make their bellies their gods; belches are their praise; all they can think of is their appetites. (Philippians 3:12-19)

But He knows the way that I take; when He has tested me, I shall come forth as gold. (Job 23:10).

No matter what comes your way, choose which direction to take. In times like these, it's your choice to make a decisive change concerning making an appropriate response to a particular situation. You cannot direct the blowing of the wind but can adjust to the changes. Turning points present an opportunity to choose moving forward into a new direction. Embracing seasonal transitions are helpful for responding positively whenever expectations inevitably meet with disappointment.

I have learned that God designs a masterpiece which cannot be duplicated; therefore, you are a unique designer original. Enjoying life is a choice and you can choose to be better or bitter; however, it doesn't mean that there aren't problems or uncomfortable situations. For the most part, transitional seasons provoke a redefining and realignment with Divine purpose. In between where you began a process and its conclusion, there can be a series of crisis or significant emotional events. The space between promise and performance call for walking by faith; this is the mystery of walking with God. He will bring you safely through every challenging situation.

You may not know how or when but be assured of His promise to always be there in the midst of it all. I will spare details of personal experiences in this regard because there have been several critical events and turning points. After enduring through many years of stormy seasons, lessons learned helped to define strategies for identifying beliefs about the world, myself and unique purpose.

Here is a glimpse of how the discovery process can be helpful in learning why you showed up on the earth. This list, by no means, was put together over night but during times of difficulties, seasons of changes, challenges and failings often. In order to identify what is believed and why, it is necessary to have clearly defined ideas of your identity so that good choices and wisdom can be applied.

Strategies for Choosing Wisely:

Self- Discovery Questions

- **Who am I?**
- **What do I want?**
- **What can I do to achieve it?**
- **Why am I here?**

Important Nuggets :

- **Recognize that you were created to fulfill a uniquely designed purpose.**
- **Recognize that you are equipped with the necessary gifts to fulfill your purpose.**

- Recognize the Lordship of Christ and surrender to His will.

- Recognize that a fulfilled life begins and ends with service to others.

- Recognize your passion for particular areas of expertise.

- Recognize that no one's unique gift is more important than another.

- Recognize that excellence in a certain area develops over a period of time.

- Recognize that success in life is contingent upon a willingness to trust and obey God's plan.

- Recognize that God's grace empowers you to manage and fulfill designed purpose.

Believe in Yourself:

- Believe you are God's masterpiece.
- Trust God's timing.
- Know and appreciate your story.
- Seek to understand and know God; His will; His ways.

- Be kind to yourself during the developmental process.
- Maintain a lifestyle of prayer, study, worship and praise.
- Stay consistent; Stay connected to Divine power source.
- Accept who God created you to be; avoid competing or comparing yourself with others.
- Learn to be comfortable with who you are (you don't have to struggle to be yourself).

It is marvelous to learn that God has been working behind the scenes along your life's journey to bring you forward at the right time, in the right place, with the right people and in the right season to work for the cause of the kingdom. Whenever you finally discover your Divine Purpose with the desire to work diligently for the glory of God, there is an eternal and redeeming value to everything you do, no matter how small or insignificant.

Let the wisdom and knowledge of Christ have the preeminence as you persevere over the long haul through multiple challenges for the glory of God. Whenever ministry takes place for the glory of God, His presence hovers over the atmosphere to bring healing, deliverance, encouragement and empowerment so that kingdom work can be continued more effectively.

For our present troubles are small and won't last very long. Yet they produce for us a glory that vastly outweighs them and will last forever! So we don't look at the troubles we can see now; rather, we fix our gaze on things that cannot be seen. For the things we see now will soon be gone, but the things we cannot see will last forever. (2 Corinthians 4:17-18)

By His Divine power, God has given us everything we need for living a godly life. We have received all of this by coming to know Him, the one who called us to Himself by means of His marvelous glory and excellence. And because of His glory and excellence, He has given us great and precious promises. These are the promises that enable you to share His divine nature and escape the world's corruption caused by human desires (2 Peter 1:3-4).

Chapter VI

Crossing Over

U nder Joshua's leadership, God's people were prepared to cross over the Jordan River into the promised territory. He obeyed God's instructions for successfully moving forward through the raging water. Whenever the people broke camp to cross the Jordan, the priests carrying the Ark of the Covenant went ahead of them (Joshua 3:1-4). People left their tents (place of familiarity/comfort level) and traveled a great distance before they could view the new territory on the other side.

Now the Jordan is at flood stage all during the harvest; the raging water is several feet above normal and is rushing quickly; it is an obstacle standing in the way between where they are and their destination. The Jordan symbolizes a place of weakness, distractions, impossibilities, (these are key tools the enemy uses to hinder forward movement). This is a time for a reality check of limitations and for making the decision whether to cross over or settle-to trust God or not.

In the space between promise and manifestation it is essential that you keep believing by faith to receive abundant blessings. This is the mystery of walking with God. Stand firmly, believing what has been promised will be fulfilled. All things are possible for those who can believe. God moves in times and seasons that are incomprehensible to finite minds. At the appointed time, you are repositioned to cross over in accordance with designed purpose.

Nevertheless, as soon as the priests who carried the Ark reached the Jordan and their feet touched the water's edge, the water from upstream stopped flowing; the people crossed over opposite Jericho. The Priests, who carried the Ark, stood firm on dry ground in the middle of the water, until all the people crossed over on dry ground. Joshua relayed the message that God had spoken, assuring them of Divine intervention to do wonders. The priests were obedient and willing to risk going forward through uncharted waters (Joshua 3:14-17, 4:21-24).

In a place of vulnerability, the enemy launches another attack that is designed to make you quit, give up, become fearful and doubtful. Enemies observe and keep a record of your spiritual progress to determine your faith level and areas of vulnerability. A place of transition/turning point or crisis, help you realize the need for God. He is well able to help you at the right time-in the right alignment with His plan. It is good to remember that you are safe and secure in His arms; therefore, you can trust and obey instructions for moving forward into a new assigned place. By remaining courageous and confident with assignment, you can choose to crossover and risk launching out into deep waters in obedience to God.

If you are willing and available, do not forget how the Lord delivered and brought you into a prosperous place. Today, faithful disciples are confronting many obstacles, intimidating or mocking forces and obstacles on every hand; but God is able to deliver out of them all.

These are times of war, crisis, political and social unrest, natural disasters, conflict and darkness all around; nevertheless, continue to trust God for deliverance out of every difficulty.

Some trust in chariots and some in horses, but we trust in the name of the Lord our God. (Psalm 20:7)

It is necessary for navigating successfully during critical times, that you show up, fully armed, prepared to make a righteous and courageous stand. The battle is not yours, it belongs to the Lord; therefore, thank God who always leads you forth victoriously. What a powerful testimony to report: "Look What the Lord has done" (Colossians 2:15; 1Corinthians 15:57; 2 Corinthians 2:14; Revelation 12:11). Let us ascend to higher levels of worship, be recharged and empowered to engage in warfare.

Day by day, step by step, be aware of surroundings-stay connected to the true power source and agree to surrender wholeheartedly to the Lord. Endeavor to move forward with joyful expectation of being approved and applauded by heaven, at the end of the day.

God does not call you according to current conditions, failures and past mistakes. He speaks to your future success (destiny); therefore, you can speak from your spiritual standing and not situations. He speaks the language of hope that encourages each one to succeed and will not leave you in darkness if you are seeking the light. However, the manner in which you have been programmed to think determines your initial response to life's situations. For example, Jeremiah, as a young man, was assured that he was chosen to be a messenger of God; therefore, it wasn't necessary for him to focus on areas of weakness or immaturity as an excuse for being unprepared for the assignment.

The word of the Lord came to me saying, "Before I formed you in the womb I knew you, before you were born I set you apart; I appointed you as a prophet to the nations." The word of the Lord came to me: "What do you see Jeremiah?" "I see the branch of an olive tree, I replied." The Lord said to me, "You have seen correctly, for I am watching to see that my word is fulfilled." (Jeremiah 1:4-5, 11-12)

Forget the former things; do not dwell on the past. See I am doing a new thing! Now it springs up; do you not perceive it? I am making a way in the desert and streams in the wasteland. The wild animals honor me, the jackals and the owls, because I provide water in the desert and streams in the wasteland, to give drink to my people, my chosen, the people I formed for myself that they may proclaim my praise. (Isaiah 43:18-21)

It is critical for success that you choose to speak well of God at all times, worship in spirit and in truth; let His praises be continually in your mouth. Give thanks at all times, spread the news about His everlasting mercy and goodness (Psalm 107:1-2). If the Lord has redeemed your life from destruction, He is worthy of all the glory, honor and praise. He is Alpha and Omega, the beginning and the end. You have His light shining amid the darkness and prophetic insight to see new beginnings. However, it is necessary to patiently wait, stay in position until your eyes can see clearly and your ears can hear the sound of His voice leading you on the right path. When you can capture a picture (vision) of light and God's goodness for your life, in the midst of dark situations, it will enable you to move forward, cross over with boldness and confidence in pursuit of divine purpose.

I am still confident of this: I will see the goodness of the Lord in the land of the living. Wait for the Lord; be strong and take heart and wait for the Lord. (Psalm 27:13-14)

The more you can see and believe, the more you can become. You must see it to be it! God births dreams and visions in order to bring revelation, illumination and inspiration. Inspiration is communicating truth and encouragement to others. To spiritually inspire is to guide, affect, or stimulate positive emotions as directed by the Holy Spirit. Through revelation, illumination and inspiration, the Spirit of the Lord calls to deeper places, revealing secrets and divine mysteries. By faith, you can decree His word that releases favor, breakthrough, strategic alignment and prosperity. You are never alone; therefore, stay encouraged and confident of His everlasting love and mercy.

Deep calls to deep in the roar of your waterfalls; all your waves and breakers have swept over me. By day the Lord directs his love, at night his song is with me—a prayer to the God of my life. (Psalm 42:7-8)

God is placing His powerful words within the mouth of His anointed bride (church) to confess that His kingdom has come. Let His will be done on earth, in each earthen vessel, as it is in Heaven. The Lord desires that you have relentless, unwavering faith manifesting in your life. All that you need is already provided, therefore, in everything that you do, let it be done for the glory and approval of Christ. In so doing, you can continue to know the love, joy and peace that are incomprehensible.

Christ within is the hope of glory (Colossians 1:27). His supernatural empowerment is opening double doors to the future as He goes before you to keep the gates open. He is making the crooked places straight, and revealing treasures that have been hidden in secret places of darkness (Isaiah 45:1-3).

Moving forward in a new season will require believing for added grace, courage and strength. If you are willing and obedient, you shall have prosperity and success. Each day you are given new mercies; God is faithful and His mercy endures forever (Lamentations 3:22-23).

Grace and peace be yours in abundance through the knowledge of God and of Jesus our Lord. His divine power has given us everything we need for life and godliness through our knowledge of him who called us by his own glory and goodness. Through these he has given us his very great and precious promises, so that through them you may participate in the divine nature and escape the corruption in the world caused by evil desires. (2 Peter 1:2-4)

You are never alone; God promises to be with you always; in Him you have an abundant life. However, lies of an enemy want you to doubt your position in the kingdom. If you listen to or agree with his lies, you won't believe that God's grace can take the place of your greatest weakness; therefore, know that you have been called out of darkness into the marvelous light (Colossians 1:13;1 Peter 2:9).

God's touch of love can resolve any questions or fear you may be struggling with, whereby, you can see things from His perspective. He imparts supernatural, empowering grace so that you can envision and receive plans for the future. The Lord sends His angels to watch over, guide, and protect, to ensure that His word comes to pass. He is a protector and a defender of the weak and continues to speak to your potential.

God demonstrated His love for the world by sending Jesus to the earth realm to seek and save those who were lost; to heal the broken and deliver all those oppressed by the devil. As it relates to circumstances and situations, He already knows the outcome. He is a master strategist and architect who builds people through an intensive process so that they are able to serve in the kingdom.

During life's turning points, as kingdom citizens, you are expected to produce good fruit that can significantly impact the lives of others in your sphere of influence.

There is always work to be done in the field, yet willing laborers are few. So very often, God calls and equips those who are totally outside of accepted power structures. He chooses vessels, according to their potential and not their weakness. You are anointed to fulfill a unique purpose; however, it is not without a fight! You will be tested and tried in various circumstances and situations to determine the level of faith that can be maintained enduring under pressure. (1 Peter 4:12, 5:10; Luke 22:31; James 1:1-2; Daniel 7:25; 2 Corinthians 2:14).

Trials and tests are designed uniquely for every one according to their divine purpose, to perfect and develop character, teach and become a spring board to the depths of God's love. In the heat of trials, you can become better acquainted with His compassion, mercy and faithfulness which prove that grace is sufficient to make you stand. Don't be alarmed at the intense trials, persecutions, for you will not be tested beyond your capacity (Matthew 25:14-15; 1Corinthians 10:13).

Although you accept the call to fulfill assigned tasks, trials and tests that occur in private are essential before being put on public display. Things change whenever you have a close encounter with the Lord (Isaiah 6:1-8). In this environment your identity and desires may change; therefore, whatever you are working on shows what you are expecting, in other words-you get what you get ready for (2 Timothy 4:7; 1 Timothy 6:12; 2 Chronicles 16:9; Job 23:10; John 4:23).

The horse is prepared for the day of battle, but victory belongs to the Lord. (Proverbs 21:31)

Chapter VII

Living on Purpose

Everyone has a unique purpose for being born; however, if you are not authentic in functioning, your divine purpose can be aborted. Discovering why you are here and for what purpose is a journey, not a destination. It involves intense preparation, processing and persevering through many seasonal changes. God uses time and pressure to create something beautiful and magnificent. You are a masterpiece that's designed for His glory.

A worldview, for the most part, is deeply affected and driven by lens and filters that determine your perception of values and belief system, whether an accurate or distorted view. Being chosen for a unique purpose is a high and noble calling that is not to be taken lightly. Although you are here on purpose, the growth and developmental process in identifying purpose can be very challenging. Although you are destined by God to be prosperous and in good health, it's your responsibility to cooperate with His plans.

Sometimes when things, in your opinion, go wrong they are very often in alignment with Divine purpose. Every obstacle, adversity can be overcome whenever you respond positively and resolve to keep moving forward. This can be an opportunity to experience God's love and power on a deeper level.

Whenever viewing uncomfortable circumstances through the lens of purpose, you can have the strength to endure under the pressure of difficult and stormy seasons. Please be encouraged and know that God is concerned about all of His people. He sees-He cares and He already knows just what to do about current situations or circumstances; therefore, if you can believe, all things are possible. Whenever challenging situations come from all sides, your faith life is forced into the open and shows its true colors.

In every season, you can always begin again, even though many upsetting things have occurred very fast.

Even though you don't choose the seasons; however, you can choose an appropriate response and see the beauty that's there. In God's time, all things are made beautiful and work together for the good of those who are called according to His purpose (Ecclesiastes 3:11; Romans 8:28).

It's encouraging to realize that everything needed pertaining to life and righteousness is already provided. Sometimes during the waiting process, you can become discouraged; however, the solution for your concerns has already been completed. Although a task may seem to be overwhelming-way over your head, trust God to intervene and download strategies for utilizing what is already available. Surrender everything you have to Him in prayer and watch multiplication take place instead of focusing on what you don't have.

Small changes over time yield great increase. For example: a mustard seed is the smallest of all seeds but grows exponentially (Mark 4:30-32). Successful people begin with small steps but have a positive outcome in mind at the end of the day. They are committed to years of discipline, consistency and perseverance.

In every situation, be thankful because lessons learned teach you how to live on purpose. During times of being challenged, know that restoration, refreshing of the soul can occur as God leads you along the right path. The insecurities experienced during challenging times help to define who you really are at the core. You are challenged most in chaos and not in comfort; therefore, continue standing strong, by faith, on the word of God. Stay focused, stay on course and stay connected to the true power source.

During times of transition- (a gap between seasons or turning points) the way you exit determines how you will enter the next season. #Pray #Praise #Press #Persevere through the difficulties of tight/narrow places with a joyful heart and hopeful expectation. Maintain an attitude of: "Not my will Lord, but Yours be done. Yes Lord, my life is Yours." He is able to make you stand.

During stormy, dark seasons with strong winds blowing in your life, causing disruptions and uncertainties, it's a time for reevaluating who you really are at the core. Your response to difficult situations or circumstances can be helpful for navigating through a vortex of doubt and discouragement.

The more excellent way to manage multiplied challenges is through obeying the greatest commandment-
love God and love one another. In so doing, Holy Spirit
helps you to become faithful and obedient servants, who
are faithful in every circumstance. Through worship,
praise and prayer, you can continually stand firm on
the promises of God; therefore, don't lose heart during
desert or wilderness seasons.

Forget the former things, do not dwell on the past.
See I am doing a new thing! Now it springs up; do you
not perceive it? I am making a way in the desert and
streams in the wasteland. (Isaiah 43:18,19)

Preparation time is not wasted time, no matter how
long the process may take. Every preparation stage is
different; however, God knows just what it will take to
prepare you for fulfillment of destiny. Throughout the
preparation process, it is critical for successful achieve-
ment to have a persevering attitude. Perseverance is the
trait that helps facilitate fulfillment of your purpose;
consequently, igniting passion that catapults you forward
to accomplish great things. Passion fuels purpose and is
a motivating factor that can help you to stay focused on
achieving desired goals and objectives.

Here's a very important Reminder: Whatever task the Lord assigns to you, even if it seems to be way over your head, just do it and leave the outcome to Him. Whenever you're challenged by fear, to the extent, giving up seems a viable option, rise up anyway, although afraid. Small changes can create big outcomes. The ending can be better than the beginning. In God's time, all things are made beautiful.

Sometimes, as a faithful disciple of Christ, there are times when instructions are misinterpreted; therefore, you can become exhausted trying to complete an assignment. It is very critical to obey specific instructions and learn to be content in every season. You cannot direct the wind but you can adjust and embrace new directions.

But may the God of all grace, who called us to His eternal glory by Christ Jesus, after you have suffered a while, perfect, establish, strengthen, and settle you. To Him be the glory and the dominion forever and ever. Amen. (I Peter 5:10-11)

This is my command—be strong and courageous! Do not be afraid or discouraged. For the Lord your God is with you wherever you go. (Joshua 1:9)

Therefore, I urge you, brothers, in view of God's mercy, to offer your bodies as a living sacrifice, holy and pleasing to God- this is your spiritual act of worship. Do not conform any longer to the pattern of this world, but be transformed by the renewing of your mind. Then you will be able to test and approve what God's will is- His good, pleasing and perfect will. (Romans 12:1-2)

Chapter VIII

Seasons

There is an opportune time to do things, a right time for everything on the earth; God made everything beautiful in itself and in its time (Ecclesiastes 3:1,11). My troubles turned out all for the best- they forced me to learn from Your textbook. Truth from Your mouth means more to me than striking it rich in a gold mine. (Psalm 119:71,72)

Characteristics of Natural Seasons:

1. Spring: Roots mature during rainy season producing growth of vegetation and beautiful flowering trees and plants.

2. **Summer: Earth points toward the sun making the earth hot with long days and short nights. Certain plants can thrive in heat: perennials, geraniums, hydrangea and impatiens....**

3. **Fall: Transition season from summer to winter. Green Leaves change to brilliant colors as a result of transformation in leaf pigments making leaves turn various colors.**

4. **Winter: Earth points away from the sun causing the weather to be cooler, days shorter and nights longer. During dormant season for plants, nutrients are stored in the roots and stems in preparation for rigorous growth in spring.**

In every season there are turning points in which there is an opportunity for choosing whether to become better or bitter. You can embrace life changes; therefore, begin again with a new perspective and identity! You don't choose the season; however, responses are determined by your positional standing and alignment with God's timing and due season (Kairos). You can choose to see beauty in every season; therefore, move whenever

God directs. Resolve to stay in step with His rhythm and don't hold on to past traumas or a comfortable place.

You can choose to cross over into a new place of favor, although challenging situations seem to increase. Remain confident and courageous because God promises to be with you every step of the way. Don't despise small things because success and significance begin with small things. Life is a journey of discovering purpose and beliefs that are painted with seasons of pain, struggles, sorrow, grief, twists, turns-all of which present an opportunity to choose an appropriate response.

Important Nuggets:

- Enjoy Every Season, however, not without fighting the good fight of faith! (1Tim. 6:12).
- Appreciate and reflect upon a collage of victories.
- Learn to wait well because waiting is an excellent teacher.
- Timing is Everything!

Life's journey presents many opportunities to learn valuable lessons in every season, even-though there could be times in which many challenges, changes, twists or turns cause you to grapple with harsh realities. In any case, there is beauty and purpose in every season because as people of faith, you have a sure and steadfast anchor of hope in Christ. You can navigate successfully during a turning point season if the choice is made to build a bridge of love and unity for going over troubled waters. There are many turning point seasons along the journey which call for change in perspectives concerning current realities. Nonetheless, no matter the situation, you can arise from dark places of trouble, enjoy your journey and begin again.

Points to Remember:

1. You can choose to see beauty in every season by making each situation meaningful.
2. Choose to live in the moment; Don't get stuck in the past or be anxious about the future.
3. Manage feelings and thoughts about experiences.
4. Remember to avoid making decisions when you are: hungry, angry, lonely or tired.
5. Change what comes out of your mouth.

Declare promises of God and pray His word. Give thanks in every season.

6. Trust/Obey/Worship Continually!
7. Believe that all things are working for your good.
8. Stand boldly by faith on Christ-the solid rock; all other ground is sinking sand.

Whenever expectations collide with disappointment, respond accordingly to your faith level.

For everything there is a season, a time for every activity under heaven. Yet God has made everything beautiful for its own time. He has planted eternity in the human heart, but even so, people cannot see the whole scope of God's work from beginning to end (Ecclesiastes 3:1,11)

Discovering beauty in a season can influence every facet of daily living, relationships, decisions and very often involves a very long process of identifying purpose or a cause worth fighting for and establishing a belief system. The process is painted by seasons of adverse winds or a multiplicity of challenges. Adversity however, provides an opportunity for you to choose an appropriate response to challenging situations while learning to wait patiently. In God's time, all things work out favorably for those who love Him and are called according to divine purpose. (Romans 8:28). Staying closely aligned with His timing helps to determine when it's your time and your turn to move forward into greater dimensions of living on purpose.

True faith, genuine faith is life transforming and is built on the word of God through Christ-a firm foundation. In these chaotic times, faithful disciples are being summoned to times of engaging in serious intercessory prayer. The glimmer and glamour of personalities, entertaining ministries, gimmicks, manipulation are fading. Now is the time for seeking The Lord in prayer for healing, rest, renewal, restoration and refreshing. Repent so that times of refreshing can come from the presence of The Lord (Acts 3:19).

There are no push button methods or shortcuts to being in holy communion with Almighty God. It is in the life-long commitment of having enduring faith that true disciples are developed and transformed to reflect the image of Christ, from glory to glory (1 Corinthians 3:18). You have the responsibility to cooperate with God in each new season in order to realize the beauty that's discovered there.

How well God must like you— you don't hang out at Sin Saloon, you don't slink along Dead-End Road, you don't go to Smart-Mouth College. Instead you thrill to GOD 's Word, you chew on Scripture day and night. You're a tree replanted in Eden, bearing fresh fruit every month, never dropping a leaf, always in blossom. (Psalm 1:3)

For if you remain silent at this time, relief and deliverance for the Jews will arise from another place, but you and your father's family will perish. And who knows but that you have come into the kingdom, for such a time as this? (Esther 4:14)

Esther Responded with prayer and fasting to obtain favor from the king, which served as an example of humility, compassion and naked prayer. God loves His people, no matter how many times they have disobeyed, wandered in a wilderness of despair, discouragement, disappointment, hopelessness, darkness or trapped in bondages of any kind.

God searches for a heart that is loyal to Him so that His mighty power to save, heal and deliver can be demonstrated (2 Chronicles 16:9). He listens to hear His people cry out for help and answers by showing great and mighty works (Jeremiah 33:1).

In discovering purpose, it is necessary to walk through difficult seasons in which many lessons can be learned. Since the plan for the journey was ordained by your creator, the master builder and chief architect, you can move forward, recognize beauty and His fingerprint in every season. There is precious treasure built within and to the extent you wholeheartedly surrender to divine purpose, this precious treasure can be discovered; whereby God is praised and glorified.

There is a cause to arise, build up broken and torn down places; shine the light of Christ into every dark place in the right season. Build up and encourage others from a position of love, rest and peace instead of frustration or criticism. In every generation, God has a remnant of faithful disciples stationed in every place that are available to hear His voice and will arise to promote the kingdom cause.

Christ established the Ecclesia-a body of believers to be joined in Holy Communion. His passion was to save with extreme measures, all of humanity. To the utmost,

Jesus saves (Hebrews 7:25). When Jesus saw people in distress, He was moved with compassion because they were scattered like sheep without a shepherd (Mark 6:34). Riding into Jerusalem before the Passover, He stopped to look over the city and wept (Luke 19:41). in the garden of Gethsemane, He persevered in prayer, accepted the assignment to be broken, crucified on a cross and shed His blood for sinful humanity.

During the season of preparation for fulfillment of His earthly assignment, He interceded for all people, prayed for unity and commanded the disciples to love one another (John 17:20-21; 13:35).

In seasons of great distress, deplorable conditions, poverty among people, God sends ordinary representatives to do extraordinary things, to broker hope and encouragement to those who are oppressed. Nehemiah was an example of an ordinary person who led the rebuilding campaign to restore a city that had been devastated.

When I heard these things, I sat down and wept. For some days I mourned and fasted and prayed before the God of heaven, he encouraged the people to rise up and build (Nehemiah 2:18, 4:14).

Growth and development training require patience to endure seasons of difficulty. God is concerned about covenant relationships in families as they work together to advance the kingdom. It's very essential to stay focused on tasks, yet being mindful of distractions or oppositional forces. Regardless of challenging seasons, the foundation built by Christ will never fail (Matthew 16:18; 1 Corinthians 3:11).

Celebrate and Enjoy Life!!!!

Reason for Life

I don't know how to say it but somehow it seems to me that maybe we are stationed where God wants us to be; that the little place I'm filling is the reason for my birth and just to do the work I do, He sent me down to earth. If God had wanted otherwise, I reckon He'd have made me just a little different, of a worse or better grade; and since God knows and understands all things of land and sea, I fancy that He placed me here, just where he wanted me.

Sometimes I get to thinking, as my labors I review, that I should like a higher place with greater things to do but I've come to the conclusion, when the envying is stilled, that the post to which God sent me is the post He wanted filled. So I plod along and struggle in the hope, when day is through, that I'm really necessary to the things God wants to do, and there isn't any service I can give, which I should scorn, for it may be just the reason God allowed that I be born. Unknown